I0820829

The Overthinker's Guide to Making Decisions

BOOKS BY JOSEPH NGUYEN:

Don't Believe Everything You Think: Why Your Thinking Is the Beginning & End of Suffering (Expanded Edition)

Beyond Thoughts: An Exploration of Who We Are Beyond Our Minds

The Art of Creating: How to Create Art That Transforms Yourself and the World

You may find my books, courses, and newsletter on my website: josephnguyen.org

The Overthinker's Guide to Making Decisions

How to Make Decisions Without Losing Your Mind

Joseph Nguyen

Authors Equity
1123 Broadway, Suite 1008
New York, New York 10010

Copyright © 2025 by Pure Intuition LLC
All rights reserved.

Edited by Cecily van Buren-Freedman
Cover design by Jared Oriel
Book design by Studiolo Secondari

The content of this book is published in the United States of America, and persons who access it agree to do so in accordance with applicable U.S. law. All opinions expressed by Joseph Nguyen ("Nguyen") in this book are solely Nguyen's opinions and may have been previously disseminated by Nguyen on the internet, in another book, or another medium. You should not treat any opinion expressed by Nguyen as a specific inducement to make a particular decision or follow a particular strategy, but only as an expression of his opinion. Neither Nguyen nor Pure Intuition LLC, its affiliates and/ or subsidiaries warrant the completeness or accuracy of the statements and opinions in the book, and it should not be relied upon as such. Nguyen, Pure Intuition LLC, its affiliates and/or subsidiaries are not under any obligation to update or correct any information provided in this book. Nguyen's statements and opinions are subject to change without notice. The content in this book is intended to be used for informational purposes only.

Neither Nguyen nor Pure Intuition LLC, its affiliates, and/or its subsidiaries guarantee any specific outcome. Strategies or opinions mentioned in this book may not be suitable for you. This material does not take into account your individual particular objectives, situation, or needs and is not intended as recommendations appropriate for you. You must make an independent decision regarding strategies or opinions mentioned in this book. It is very important to do your own analysis before making any decision. Before acting on information or opinions in this book, you should consider whether it is suitable for your particular circumstances and strongly consider seeking advice from your own medical professional or advisor.

Library of Congress Control Number: 2025941029
Print ISBN 9798893310665
Ebook ISBN 9798893310825

Printed in the United States of America
First Printing

www.authorsequity.com

Most Authors Equity books are available at a discount when purchased in quantity for sales promotions or corporate use. Special editions, which include personalized covers, excerpts, and corporate imprints, can be created when purchased in large quantities. For more information, please email info@authorsequity.com.

Contents

I.

A New Way to Decide

Rethinking Everything We Know About Making Decisions

"Choices are the hinges of destiny."

—EDWIN MARKHAM

"We need to accept that we won't always make the right decisions, that we'll screw up royally sometimes—understanding that failure is not the opposite of success, it's part of success."

—ARIANNA HUFFINGTON

Chapter 1

The Silent Weight of Choice

"When something bad happens you have three choices. You can either let it define you, let it destroy you, or you can let it strengthen you."

—DR. SEUSS

One of the greatest powers we possess is choice, the ability to consciously choose one path over another. With this, we hold the power to reshape the course of our lives in an instant—something few, if any, other life-forms appear to do in the same way.

But with this great power comes great suffering.

Far too easily, we find ourselves trapped in indecision, a paralysis caused not by limitation, but by infinite possibility. The culprit is not too little choice, but too much. And so, we end up suffering, not because we lack options, but because we drown in them.

Heavy is the head that wears the crown of choice.

The pressure to make the *right* decision can feel overwhelming, not because the choice is impossibly complex, but because the stakes of choosing wrong feel so high. In these moments, what we feel is determined not by the size of the decision, but by the gravity of our emotions. When the mind spirals, even the smallest choice can feel like a heavy burden, as if so much depends on it.

What begins as a simple decision doesn't stay that way for long. As we contemplate different outcomes, our mind fixates on the negative. One wrong decision, we realize, and everything could fall apart—the job we worked so hard for, the love we were just beginning to trust, the fragile peace we fought to find, the chance we thought might change everything.

But it's not just bad outcomes we fear; it's the perception of others. The silence in the room. The shift in someone's tone. The look in their eyes when they no longer see us the same.

What if we lose their respect? What if we lose their love? What if the people we care about most no longer believe in us?

We can see it unfolding in our mind's eye as clear as day: choose "wrong," and suddenly the job disappears, the relationship crumbles, our reputation shatters, and the voice in our head taunts: *See? You never deserved this.*

That's the risk that feels the highest—not the practical consequence, but the way a bad decision seems to serve as evidence of our deepest fears about ourselves. A "wrong" decision doesn't just feel like a mistake; it feels like confirmation. Confirmation that we're not capable enough. Not wise enough. Not enough.

Before we know it, the worry has spiraled out of control, and what may have started as a small decision has now become an existential crisis.

And so, we find ourselves seeking advice, not necessarily for clarity, but for reassurance. Maybe if enough people tell us what to do, the weight of choosing will disappear. We silently hope—perhaps without even realizing it—that someone else will decide for us. Because if the choice ends up being a mistake, it won't be our fault, it will be theirs. After all, it's far easier to live resenting someone else's decision than it is to bear the consequences of our own.

But the more we rely on these opinions, the heavier the decision becomes. Now, in addition to the need to make the "right" choice, we must contend with the pressure to please.

This is how the burden grows. You weigh your desires against the expectations of others, feeling the quiet guilt of all they've given you. How could you possibly choose a path they don't agree with? How could you risk disappointing the very people who have supported you? It's easy to convince yourself that prioritizing what feels right for you is selfish.

And yet, if making everyone else happy were the key to your own happiness, wouldn't it have worked by now?

The truth is that the more voices we invite in, the quieter our internal voice becomes.

Each opinion, no matter how well intended, pulls us further from the still, inner knowing we already sense.

Everyone offers what they think is best, yet none of them can tell you what is best *for you*. The more we rely on others, the less we trust ourselves—and the more we begin to live a life curated for approval, not alignment.

Most people give advice based on *their fears, regrets, and limitations*. They see the world through the lens of their past, not your future. Their doubts are not your destiny. Their wounds are not your path. Their beliefs are not your truth.

No one else knows you better than you. No one else carries the same passions, desires, or dreams as you. Others will tell you what *they* would do, but they cannot tell you what is *right for you*.

The cost of trying to make everyone around you happy is your own happiness.

But here's the good news: just because things *have* been a certain way doesn't mean they *have to stay* that way.

Frank Sonnenberg said, "Lessons in life will be repeated until they are learned." But how can we learn the lesson if no one shows us another way? We can't choose a new path until we realize there *is* one.

My hope for this guide is that it helps you to see life differently—to stop overthinking your decisions, to trust yourself again, and to find the courage to create a life that feels true to *you*.

Chapter 2

Why Do We Overthink?

"A decision made from fear is always the wrong decision."

—TONY ROBBINS

You don't overthink because something is wrong with you. You overthink because something *matters* to you.

Because you care. Because there's meaning wrapped in the moment. Because somewhere inside, you sense that this choice might shape your future—your identity, your safety, your connection to others.

But the root of overthinking is not care. It's fear.

Not the kind of fear that punches through your chest and announces itself in panic. It's the subtle kind. The kind that disguises itself as responsibility. The kind that whispers in the back of your mind: *What if you make the wrong choice? What if you can't handle what comes next? What if this is the thing that finally exposes you as not enough?*

If decisions were only logical, we wouldn't experience indecision. We'd weigh the pros and cons, make a choice, and move forward without giving it a second thought. But decisions aren't just calculations, they're mirrors. They show us who we think we are and who we're afraid we might be.

It's never just about *Which path should I take*. It's *What will it say about me if I make this choice? Will I still be loved, respected, safe, and successful?*

All overthinking—no matter the surface story—can be traced back to fear. Fear of failure. Fear of regret. Fear of disappointing others. Fear of not being who we think we should be.

And yet, overthinking doesn't mean something is wrong with your mind. It's evidence of a mind trying to protect you from these fears.

It builds mental simulations, plays out every scenario, and calculates every angle, not to find the truth—although it may feel this way—but to find control.

Control over pain. Control over loss. Control over how others see you.

But the allure of control is an illusion. Here's the paradox: the more we try to control, the more afraid we become and the less free we feel. It's like psychological quicksand—the more we struggle, the faster we sink into fear, self-doubt, and paralysis.

And so, the way out is not through grasping for control, but through acceptance. When you recognize and face fear, you don't give it power. You take it back. Because once you see fear clearly—not as truth, but as a pattern—it loosens its grip.

The moment you stop running from fear, it stops running your life.

Solving overthinking doesn't require another plan, another pro/con list, or another round of mental gymnastics. It requires your presence. Your grounded, clear-eyed willingness to feel what you've been avoiding.

This is the turning point.

Once you realize that all overthinking is just fear in disguise, you can stop battling every thought and simply address the root emotion.

And that's when a new possibility emerges: What if everything we've been taught about fear is backward? What if fear meant not that something was wrong but that you were on the verge of something right?

Think back—how many times was fear loudest right before you chose something that changed you for the better? The fear wasn't the problem, it was just your soul pointing to what you'd been searching for and what you were ready for all along.

What if fear was just a signal that something important is surfacing—a place within us still holding on to the illusion that our worth is conditional?

What if it was your soul letting you know what would help you grow the most?

Chapter 3

Your Focus Determines Your Decisions

"May your choices reflect your hopes, not your fears."

—NELSON MANDELA

Long before we had therapy, coaching, or neuroscience, humans understood something essential: that the mind contains many voices. Some bring clarity, and others bring confusion.

And that what determines our path is not which voice speaks the loudest but *which one we choose to listen to.* This isn't just a metaphor; it's how the mind works. Especially in moments of uncertainty, when fear and hope both speak at once.

There is a story often attributed to Cherokee tradition that depicts this universal human experience that has been passed down for generations. It lives on in moments like this—when fear and trust wrestle inside us for control.

An old man is teaching his grandson about life...

"A terrible fight is going on inside me," he tells the boy. "It is between two wolves. One is fear, envy, sorrow, regret, greed, and self-doubt. The other is joy, peace, love, hope, and confidence. The same fight is going on inside you—and inside every person, too."

The grandson thinks for a moment and asks, "Which wolf will win?"

The old man simply replies, "The one you feed."

Overcoming fear doesn't come from fighting it. The more you resist or avoid fear, the more you fan the flames of fear itself. Because resistance is still a form of attention, and attention is fuel. Trying to wrestle fear down is like throwing kindling on a blaze you're desperate to extinguish—it only makes it roar louder.

Fear is like fire: it doesn't die through struggle. It dies when you remove what keeps it alive.

What oxygen is to fire, your attention is to fear.

Remove the oxygen, and the flames go out.

Withdraw your attention from fear, and it begins to extinguish.

It doesn't need to be solved. It just needs to be seen for what it is.

You don't need to fight fear. You only need to *stop feeding it.*

The reality is that the emotion we make a decision from is the emotion we reinforce. This is because where our attention goes, energy flows. And where energy flows, things grow.

When we choose out of fear—fear of failure, rejection, or loss—we don't escape it; we perpetuate it.

When we focus on what we *don't* want, instead of avoiding it, we feed it. It grows until it overwhelms the decision-making process, keeping us trapped in a reactive, fight-or-flight state.

And yet, while it may be tempting to therefore think that the solution lies in minimizing emotion in general, we don't want to strip emotion from decision-making entirely. If we remove all emotion, we lose the "*good*" emotions that are crucial to decision-making as well: the hopes, the dreams, the desires, and the excitement.

This occurrence is why the goal isn't to eliminate emotion but to shift where we place our focus. So the decision becomes not about avoiding what we *don't* want but about moving toward what we *do* want.

When learning how to ski, the best instructors teach one simple rule: look where you want to go, not at the obstacles you wish to avoid. The moment you fixate on the trees, you veer toward them, and your likelihood of crashing into one increases. Not because they magically pull you in, but because your focus leads you there. **Your focus is a mental magnet.** It quietly draws you closer to whatever you give your attention to, whether it's the barriers you fear or the path you long to follow.

The same is true for decisions. When all your energy is spent trying to avoid the worst-case scenario, you don't move forward; you move *toward* the very thing you're trying to escape. You see only the barriers and lose sight of the way through.

The mind does not show us the world as it is—it shows us the world through the lens of what we expect to see. This experience is confirmation bias in action. When we fixate on fear, we train our minds to find more of it. When we believe something will go wrong, our brains search for proof, and we will always find evidence to support what we choose to believe. It filters reality to align with what we already expect, reinforcing the very patterns we're trying to escape.

This is why refocusing our attention isn't about ignoring reality; it's about *expanding our perception of it* so that we don't live a life formed only by fear and the negative. It's about fully accepting what is while seeing beyond it—recognizing new possibilities instead of unconsciously repeating old patterns.

By widening our lens, we don't reject the world as it is; we evolve beyond the limitations of how we once saw it. We give ourselves **permission to make decisions based on what we *want* instead of just avoiding what we fear.**

The same mechanism that keeps us stuck is the one that can set us free. Instead of focusing on the fear in a decision, focus on the possibility, and your mind will make choices that work to make your dreams a reality. Focus on what you want, and you will naturally begin to move toward it.

Make decisions based on how you *want* to feel rather than on what you're *afraid* to experience, and your life will be shaped by your dreams instead of your fears.

Attention is the architect of your reality.

The mind is fertile soil, and emotions are the seeds planted within it. Your attention is the water that brings them to life. Whatever you nourish—fear or love, doubt or confidence—will take root and grow. The mind does not discriminate; it breeds what you feed it.

If you make decisions to avoid fear, you are watering the weeds of worry, allowing them to spread and take over. But if you make decisions to cultivate peace, love, and joy, you are tending to a garden of growth and expansion, where each decision plants the future you want to live in.

The soil does not choose what grows. *You do.*

Chapter 4

Where Our Best Decisions Come From

"The best decisions aren't made with your mind, but with your Instinct."

—LIONEL MESSI

Recall a decision that profoundly changed your life for the better. Maybe it was moving to a new city, changing careers, pursuing a passion, or starting/ending a relationship. Choosing to take care of your health. Starting a business or writing a book.

When you made the decision, was it purely logical, or was there something deeper at play? Did you weigh every opinion, seeking external validation, or did you trust yourself despite the uncertainty? Was it driven by fear and safety, or did it feel like stepping into something bigger than yourself? Did you make it to meet expectations, or did it come from a sense of alignment and inner truth?

More likely than not, this life-altering decision wasn't the safest, most rational, most socially acceptable choice.

It didn't come from the part of you obsessed with control, certainty, and minimizing risk. It came from focusing on your hopes and dreams, from what you imagined your life could be. It came from somewhere beyond opinions, beyond fear, beyond logic—it came from *you.*

Not the version of you conditioned to conform. Not the version of you that prioritizes security over growth. But the *real* you. The one that knows, deep down, that growth—not comfort—is the path to a life of meaning, peace, and fulfillment.

Your best decisions don't come from the mind that hesitates, overthinks, and asks, *What will other people think of me? What if it doesn't work out?*

They come from the part of you that feels, *What is my heart saying I'm meant to do? What would I choose if I weren't afraid? What feels undeniably right, even if it doesn't make sense yet? What am I unexplainably pulled toward?*

This is your intuition speaking, and it is who you truly are—the part of you that sees beyond fear and into possibility. The part of you that recognizes that real security comes not from playing small but from stepping fully into alignment with who you were meant to be.

The only filter that matters when making choices is this:

Will it contract who you are or expand who you're becoming?

Because the truth is, the best decisions of your life will never be found in the logic of the mind. They will be felt in the *knowing* of your heart.

This doesn't mean you should ignore knowledge or act without understanding. Gathering information matters, but only to the point where it brings you greater clarity, not greater confusion. There's a moment when seeking more shifts from empowering you to paralyzing you. You'll know you've reached that point when additional thinking doesn't create more certainty but instead deepens your confusion and doubt. That's when it's time to stop asking your mind and start trusting what you already know deep down.

Your best decisions come from trusting yourself. From listening to that still, small voice inside—the one only *you* can hear. From following what you *know* to be true, even when it doesn't make sense to others. From choosing your heart over your fear, and alignment over approval.

Not because it keeps you safe. But because it sets you *free*.

Chapter 5

But What If I Make the Wrong Decision by Trusting Myself?

"Sometimes you make the right decision, sometimes you make the decision right."

—PHIL MCGRAW

There is an ancient Chinese story from the second century BCE that beautifully illustrates why we shouldn't rush to label events as ultimately "good" or "bad" and reveals the philosophical truth that all situations are constantly evolving.

The Story of the Wise Farmer

There was once an old farmer who lived on the border of an ancient kingdom. He was known not for his wealth or his status but for the way he responded to life, as if he saw something the rest of the village missed.

One day, his only horse broke free and ran away across the hills.

The neighbors rushed over: "What terrible news! This is such bad luck."

The old farmer just said, "Maybe. We'll see."

A few weeks later, the horse returned, and behind it trailed a group of wild stallions.

Now the neighbors came running again.

"What incredible luck! You've multiplied your fortune!"

Again, the old farmer said, "Maybe. We'll see."

His son, young and full of fire, tried to tame one of the new horses. But the horse bucked and threw him hard to the ground.

His leg was badly broken.

The neighbors shook their heads. "What a tragedy. Your poor son."

The old farmer only said, "Maybe. We'll see."

Months passed, and the kingdom fell into war. Soldiers came to draft every able-bodied young man.

But the farmer's son was spared because his broken leg made him unfit for battle.

> Most of the other young men never returned home.
>
> The villagers were quiet this time.

We're taught to label things as *right* or *wrong*, *good* or *bad*, *successes* or *failures*—as if life is that absolute. But the truth is: Outcomes are rarely what we expect, and we don't know enough to judge all that will come from one decision.

At the moment when you make a decision, it is too soon to tell all the effects it will have. Some will be good, some will be bad, and most will be impossible to predict. A decision you regret today might be the very thing that leads to a discovery tomorrow. A path that feels unclear or difficult might be clearing away something that wasn't serving you.

Most events in life aren't entirely good or bad—they often hold the potential for both, depending on how we relate to them.

Take a volcanic eruption, for example. To those nearby, it may bring destruction, loss, and upheaval. But over time, that same eruption enriches the soil, creating some of the most fertile land on earth. Entire ecosystems return, more vibrant than before.

So is the eruption a tragedy or a necessity? The event itself doesn't decide that; we do. To the earth, it isn't good or bad; it simply is. It's a process, not a judgment. It's not the eruption that carries meaning; but the label we give it and the narrative we create about it in our minds.

And in that way, it reflects a larger truth: all events are inherently neutral. *We* are the ones who assign meaning, and the label we give determines how we feel about a situation. This isn't meant to dismiss the reality of pain. There are countless deeply difficult, heartbreaking, tragic events in this world. But it's important to recognize that even in those moments, our labels can either weigh us down or help us rise.

This is how it is with decisions, too. Think back to a decision you consider "good." Did it only bring positive outcomes? Or did it come with a cost? A door closed, a connection altered, a part of you quietly wondering, even now, about a different path.

Now recall a decision you labeled "bad." Did it only lead to regret? Or did it push you to grow, reveal your strengths, or guide you to something better that you couldn't have planned?

Most decisions lead to a mix of outcomes—some expected, some not. Yet we often judge the decision itself as absolutely good or bad based solely on how the story has played out *so far*.

Even with the most thoughtful, carefully planned decisions, we never have full control over how they turn out. Which means that our power lies not in whether the decision works out exactly the way we hoped but in how we respond.

The truth is that how we feel about a decision is shaped much less by the outcome itself than by the meaning we assign to it.

Sometimes, the most powerful shift begins with simply releasing the story you've been telling yourself. Letting go of the negative response—*"this shouldn't have happened," "this was wrong"*—doesn't mean denying the pain. It means we stop adding to it with the weight of judgment.

When you're not acting from harm, there are no inherently "wrong" decisions.

There are no perfect paths, just as there are no perfect decisions. Only choices that limit or expand who you are. Only decisions that are unaligned or aligned with who you are becoming.

And the beautiful part is: You can *feel* the difference. Your body knows. Your breath knows.

When you make decisions out of fear, anxiety, or the need for approval, something inside you tightens. That tightening is often a sign that you're making decisions from the *outside in*—letting outcomes, expectations, or other people's opinions dictate your direction. And when you do that, you place your ability to find peace in the hands of things entirely beyond your control.

But when you make choices from the *inside out*—guided by alignment, intuition, and your quiet knowing—something softens and expands. Even if it's uncomfortable or uncertain, there's a sense of lightness, of truth, of coming home to yourself. You stop chasing the "right" outcome and start honoring what's *right for you.*

The more we ground our decisions in inner truth, the more we begin to realize: **There are no failures, only**

invitations to grow. No path is wasted. Every decision offers something we need, whether it's clarity, healing, strength, or the reminder to listen more closely next time.

When growth becomes the goal, fear begins to dissolve. In doing so, you release the pressure to choose the perfect path and become the person who can walk any path with presence, courage, and peace.

This is where real confidence is born—not from trying to *control* the future, but from knowing that you can *weather any* future.

When your peace is rooted in how you meet life—not in what life gives you—you begin to trust something far more powerful than control.

You begin to trust your ability to stay centered in uncertainty. To adapt, respond, and evolve.

You stop spiraling when plans fall apart.

You stop second-guessing every step.

You still feel the fear, but it no longer decides for you. Discomfort isn't a problem to solve; it's a signal you're on the right path. It's a sign not of weakness but of growth. And it's proof that you're no longer avoiding who you're meant to become.

It's a sign that you are a person who trusts that even if things go sideways, you'll find your way back. Not because the path is perfect, but because you know how to listen.

Not because everything goes right, but because *you no longer need it to.*

Think of life as a compass.

You don't need to know every twist and turn to get to your destination. You only need to take the next step and trust that your inner guidance will lead you from there. And if you take a detour, the compass doesn't scold you. It doesn't criticize, shame, or call you foolish for taking a wrong turn. It simply points you north so you can find your way back again. You don't need to panic if you make a "wrong turn"; you can always course correct.

Your inner guidance never makes you question your worth.

We are the ones who do.

Life doesn't demand perfection.

We are the ones who do.

Your inner compass—your intuition, your deeper knowing—only ever wants to guide you to where you're meant to be. No matter how many turns it takes.

And truthfully, there is no path without obstacles.

No road without bumps.

No journey without unexpected delays.

So the goal isn't to pick the perfect path. It's to become the person who trusts themselves enough to navigate *any* path. Some paths will be smoother. Some will be rougher. Others are more scenic. But all of them will take you where you're meant to go—as long as you keep choosing what feels true to you.

And remember, no decision is final. You're not locked into any one path forever.

You're allowed to change. To grow. To *outgrow* who you've been and choose a version of yourself that feels more alive, more free, more whole.

You don't have to get every decision right to get there. You're going to make mistakes no matter what. But when you make decisions that feel true to you, you reclaim not just your power, but your peace.

And when you listen to your inner voice, you gain something far greater than just options—you gain freedom, including the freedom to make mistakes.

There is no learning without mistakes.

No growth without discomfort.

No enlightenment without suffering.

They're all sides of the same coin.

If it's true that you can't avoid the inevitable obstacles of life no matter which path you choose, you may as well live a life of liberation on your terms.

You've spent your life trying to avoid the wrong choice. But what if the only mistake was believing you weren't strong enough to navigate whatever life has in store?

Chapter 6

What If My Decision Upsets Someone I Care About?

"One of the greatest regrets in life is being what others would want you to be, rather than being yourself."

—SHANNON L. ALDER

Sometimes, your decisions will upset others. There is always someone who will disagree and disapprove of what you choose to do with your life. But that doesn't necessarily mean you made the wrong choice—it may simply mean that you're choosing to honor your truth instead of their expectations. And for some people, that will feel uncomfortable, especially if they've become accustomed to your self-abandonment.

We're often conditioned—through culture, family, work, or even friends—to believe that being a "good" person means keeping the peace, minimizing conflict, and making sure others feel okay, even if it costs us our peace. We mistake approval for happiness, thinking that if we just make the "right" choice in the eyes of others, we will finally feel whole.

But no amount of outside validation will ever make you feel like you're enough. And over time, that constant pleasing begins to hollow us out. It disconnects us from ourselves and places our sense of self-worth in the hands of other people's approval.

When you prioritize other people's opinions and desires over your truth, you begin to lose sight of who you are. You become an echo of others' expectations, an empty vessel hoping to be filled with their approval.

But here's the truth most of us were never taught:

Your peace does not need to be sacrificed for someone else's comfort.

And someone else's comfort should never come at the expense of your growth, your joy, or your sense of alignment.

Their reaction is not your responsibility—but your integrity is.

And the real question is not "What if they're upset?" but rather: "What is more important—your peace or their approval?"

The best thing you can ask from others is their support, not their validation. Their perspective, not their permission.

If someone makes you feel guilty for choosing what is true and life-giving for you—if they are upset that you are choosing joy, growth, or rest—you have to gently ask yourself:

Do they truly want me to be happy, or do they want me to keep them happy at the cost of my happiness?

It's easy to confuse guilt with wrongdoing. But feeling guilty is often just an echo of old conditioning, not proof that you've made a mistake. Especially when your decision isn't causing harm but simply disappointing someone who benefits from your self-sacrifice.

People who love you *conditionally* will want you to choose them, even if it means abandoning yourself.

People who love you *unconditionally* will want you to choose what makes you come alive—even if it challenges them, even if it changes the relationship, even if it means letting go of their idea of who they thought you were.

This doesn't mean you should cut people off or harden your heart. It doesn't mean you should burn bridges and justify it as empowerment. It means you can learn to hold compassion and boundaries at the same time. You can stay kind while staying true to yourself. You can remain loving while being honest about what no longer works.

At the end of the day, relationships will change as you do. Some may fall away—not because you were too much, but because you stopped being too little.

If that happens, it's not a loss. It's a gentle, purposeful pruning of your life that releases what no longer serves you. A spiritual shedding of who you once were, so that you can make space for who you're becoming.

And if that makes someone angry, it doesn't mean something is wrong with you. Anger is often grief in disguise—a mourning for the version of you they were attached to, the version who said yes when you meant no. And that grief may come out as blame, guilt, or withdrawal.

You can honor their grief without collapsing into it.

You can hold space for their pain without sacrificing your becoming.

You're allowed to keep growing, even if they don't understand yet.

And you can love them through their process without losing yourself in it.

The most loving thing you can do in those moments is to reassure them that your love for them hasn't disappeared. It's just evolving. It may no longer look the way they expected, but it can still be real. It can still be kind. It can still be love.

You can tend to their feelings, explaining your decision and offering emotional support as you help them work through their reaction. But you can do this without letting their emotions determine or override your decisions.

Trying to keep everyone happy is a subconscious attempt to control what you cannot. And it's one of the surest ways to suffer because it keeps your sense of self-worth tied to other people's emotional states, which you were never meant to carry.

The people who truly love you—*not just who you've been for them, but who you are in your essence*—will want you to feel whole. Not just agreeable. Not just convenient. But fulfilled, expressed, and free.

Sometimes, the most loving thing you can do for someone else is to stop living your life to make them happy—because it gives them permission to do the same. And sometimes, the most loving thing you can do for yourself is to let go of the version of you who lived in fear of disappointing others.

True love doesn't trap you in obligation.

It invites you into freedom.

And freedom will often ask you to disappoint others so that you no longer disappoint yourself.

Chapter 7

So How Do We Actually Make Better Decisions?

"Decision is a risk rooted in the courage of being free."

—PAUL TILLICH

As we explored earlier, the way we feel about our decisions—before, during, and after making them—is shaped by *how* we make them. When we choose from fear—trying to avoid regret, loss, or judgment—we only end up strengthening the very fear we hoped to escape.

But when we shift our focus from what we *don't* want to what we *do* want to experience, when we move from fear to trust, from avoidance to alignment, something subtle but profound begins to change. We stop reacting and we start creating.

Because our experience of reality is not something we passively observe. It's something we actively shape. It is not fixed; it's *fluid*. Every choice is a brushstroke on the canvas of our existence, and the more we choose from fear, the more we paint in the colors of limitation.

But the opposite is also true.

There are deeper voices that call to us—quietly, consistently—beneath all the noise: a desire for peace, a sense of truth, the pull to grow, and the longing to live with more love and possibility.

We don't often name them. We rarely prioritize them. But when we choose from these places, we begin to live differently.

They're not just ideas but ways of being we long for and are meant to live from.

This type of decision is what we'll call an *actualized decision*.

An actualized decision is a choice made not from fear, pressure, or the need for approval, but from self-trust, alignment, presence, and love.

Sometimes, the most aligned decision feels scary—not because it's wrong, but because it invites you to outgrow the limits you once needed to feel safe.

It doesn't guarantee success, but it brings peace in the midst of uncertainty.

The best decisions aren't made from stress and panic. They're made when you feel safe, centered, and present. Counterintuitively, by letting go of our attachment to outcomes, we give ourselves the greatest chance of making the best decision possible.

Psychologist Abraham Maslow once described a hierarchy of human needs, from the most basic (like food and safety) to the highest: self-actualization—the full expression of our potential and truest self. A state in which your thoughts, actions, and values begin to reflect who you truly are—beneath fear, conditioning, or external expectation.

An actualized decision emerges from that same place.

The Dimensions of an Actualized Decision

If we stop choosing from fear, we need a different guide to replace it. And that's where most people get stuck because we were never taught how to recognize more than a *safe* decision. But to make this shift, we need to learn to recognize how to make an *aligned* one.

Instead of asking, *"What's the right choice?"*

We need to ask: **"What kind of life do I want to create with this choice?"**

And from that place, we begin choosing with intention.

The deeper experiences we long for—peace, alignment, growth, and abundance—aren't just abstract ideals. They are the foundation of a new way of choosing: what we'll call the four dimensions of an *actualized decision*.

To make them easy to remember, they form the acronym **SAGE:**

- ▷ **Serenity**—Which choice will give me the deepest peace?
- ▷ **Alignment**—Which choice aligns with who I want to become?
- ▷ **Growth**—Which choice expands me the most?

- **Emotion**—Which choice is driven by love and abundance rather than fear?

This isn't a checklist to complete. It's a compass, one that helps you stay aligned and gently brings you back when you've strayed. Let it guide you, not to the "right" answer, but to the one that aligns with who you're here to become.

And like any true compass, it doesn't criticize when you take a wrong turn. It doesn't shame you for getting lost or punish you for changing course. It simply recalibrates—quietly, patiently—offering you a new way forward from exactly where you are.

Even when the road is unclear, even when you can't see what's ahead, this compass remains. It doesn't demand perfection.

It offers presence.

And the more you learn to trust it, the more you realize: you were never off track.

Never behind. Never broken.

Just momentarily disconnected from your own knowing. Because there's peace in remembering there is no perfect path.

And when you step back and look at the map of your life, you'll see that every turn—every detour, every delay, every decision—was leading you to the same place all along:

Back home to yourself.

Chapter 8

The TRUST Decision-Making Framework

"Your heart knows the way. Run in that direction."

—RUMI

Now that you understand the philosophy of making decisions, let's distill it into a simple, practical, and memorable framework you can use every day. The TRUST Decision-Making Framework is a five-step practice designed to help you break through overthinking and make actualized decisions that are aligned with who you are and who you're becoming. This framework is the step-by-step process for how we apply SAGE to our daily decisions, no matter how big or small. When you find yourself spiraling in indecision, stuck in a loop of what-ifs and worst-case scenarios, pause, breathe, and walk yourself through this process.

The TRUST Framework isn't meant to give you the "right" answer. It's intended to help you remember that *you already know*: that knowledge has just been buried beneath fear, noise, and pressure. It's designed to help you leave behind the fear and anxiety of overthinking and make decisions from a place of peace and intuition.

Overthinking doesn't mean something is wrong with you. It means your nervous system is overwhelmed and your mind; is trying to protect you the only way it knows how—by reaching for control. But attempting to control what we cannot doesn't create clarity; it creates overwhelm. And so this framework isn't about fighting the mind; it's about gently redirecting it toward something deeper: your truth.

As you go through each step, answer the questions as honestly and compassionately as you can. Suspend judgment—of yourself, your circumstances, and your uncertainty. Judgment doesn't bring clarity; it only keeps you stuck in fear.

By the end of this process, you won't just have an answer. You'll have something far more powerful: a decision that feels *true.* One that comes not from fear or people-pleasing but from clarity, alignment, and trust in yourself.

T—Take Five Deep Breaths

Before anything else, come home to your body. Overthinking is often a sign that you're stuck in your head, disconnected from your inner wisdom.

Taking five deep, intentional breaths activates your parasympathetic nervous system, grounds you in the present moment, and begins to calm the storm. It's the first step in shifting from reaction to clarity—from fear to truth.

You don't make great decisions in a panic. You make them when you feel safe, centered, and present.

PRACTICE:

- Regulate the nervous system by taking five slow, deep breaths.
- Try the two-to-one breathing technique: inhale for four seconds, and exhale for eight.

R—Reveal the Root Decision

When we're overwhelmed, we often lose sight of the actual decision we're trying to make. Our minds spiral into endless hypotheticals, and the choice balloons until it becomes something much larger than the actual decision at hand.

Instead of getting lost in the noise, zoom in: *What is the real decision here?*

Don't confuse the symptoms with the cause. For example, if you're considering leaving your job, your mind might be preoccupied with what your boss will think, whether your coworkers will be disappointed, or if you'll find another job in time. But all of that is just noise.

Strip it back. The root decision is: *Do I stay, or do I go?* Naming the real decision brings relief and is the first step to clarity. Simplicity cuts through confusion.

PRACTICE:

- State the decision you are facing in one clear sentence. Don't include the possible outcomes or emotions, just the decision at hand *(e.g., "Stay in this job or leave?")*.
- What event prompted this decision *(e.g., "My boss criticized my work")?*

U—Uncover the Fear and the Cost of Listening to It

At the root of overthinking is fear. Not the loud kind that screams danger, but the quieter kind that disguises itself in responsibility, doubt, and control. To move past it, we first have to name it.

What fear is this decision bringing up? What are you afraid it will mean if you choose wrong? Naming fear doesn't give it power—it reclaims your own. Once you see fear clearly, it begins to loosen its hold. And when you understand why you overthink, letting go becomes natural.

But fear of a bad outcome isn't the only thing that paralyzes us. It's the meaning we attach to the outcome that makes the fear so heavy. It's not just, *"I might fail."* It's, *"If I fail, it will mean I'm not good enough."* The story we tell ourselves is what traps us. If we can spot the story—not as truth but as a habit that no longer serves us—we can begin to dissolve it.

But stories that have lived inside us for years aren't dismantled by logic alone. Their roots go deep, and they hold on until we recognize the real cost of believing them. Fear demands a high price: our peace, our time, our confidence, our dreams. Ask yourself: What has fear already taken from me? If I keep listening to it, where will I be a year from now? Five years? Ten?

We are often more moved by the pain of what we're losing than the promise of what we could gain. When you see clearly what fear has already taken—and what it will continue to take—you find a deeper kind of courage. A strength that rises not because you're fearless but because you're no longer willing to trade your life for the illusion of safety.

At some point, the cost of playing it safe becomes greater than the risk of being true to yourself—and that is a decision not of the mind but of the soul.

PRACTICE:

- What are you afraid might happen if you choose wrong? What do you worry that choosing wrong would mean about you *(e.g., "I'll fail," "I'm not good enough")?*
- What is this fear costing you *(e.g., "Constantly seeking validation is eroding my self-confidence")?*

S—Shift from Fear to Intuition

Here's where everything changes.

If all fear vanished—if every voice of doubt and expectation and judgment disappeared—*what would you choose?*

What feels most expansive?

Shift your focus to the emotions you wish to cultivate. What possibility is most exciting to you? What choice contains more peace, freedom, love, or joy?

Let your intuition speak. Let it lead. Listen to your inner

voice, not the voices of others—even if they're well-intentioned. This is how you move from outside-in decision-making to inside-out. From reaction to alignment. From contraction to expansion.

You'll often feel this as a subtle shift—not fireworks, but a breath of relief. A loosening in the chest. A softening in your jaw. A feeling of being less at war with yourself.

Remember that there are inherently no good or bad, right or wrong decisions. Only ones that are aligned or unaligned with who you are. Your future is determined much less by the outcome than by your response to it. True confidence comes not from trying to control what happens but from trusting you can navigate whatever happens.

When in doubt, ask: *Which decision feels rooted in fear? Which one feels rooted in love and expansion?*

PRACTICE:

- ▷ Using the principles of SAGE, which choice will bring the most long-term peace, alignment, and growth—even if it feels scary to choose?
- ▷ Suspend judgment and give yourself permission to consider this choice an actual possibility. How would it feel to choose this option?
- ▷ If you release your attachment to outcomes and trust you can navigate whatever happens, what is your intuition telling you to choose?
- ▷ Write down your actualized decision.

T—Take the Smallest Possible Action

We often freeze, not because the decision is wrong, but because it feels too big, too scary to confront.

The antidote? Shrink it.

Ask yourself: *What is the smallest possible step I can take right now? One that's so doable it feels almost silly not to do it.*

Not making the whole career change, just updating your resume.

Not writing the whole book, just starting the first sentence.

Not completing the full workout, just showing up at the gym.

The goal isn't to finish. It's to begin.

Because once you move, you're no longer stuck; you're becoming.

PRACTICE:

- What's the first small step you can take that will make this choice a reality?

TRUST Decision-Making Framework

1. Take Five Deep Breaths
   - ▹ Regulate the nervous system by taking five slow, deep breaths. Try the two-to-one breathing technique: inhale for four seconds, and exhale for eight.
2. Reveal the Root Decision
   - ▹ State the decision you are facing in one clear sentence. Don't include the possible outcomes or emotions, just the decision at hand.
   - ▹ What event prompted this decision?
3. Uncover the Fear & Its Cost
   - ▹ What are you afraid might happen if you choose wrong? What do you worry that choosing wrong would mean about you?
   - ▹ What is this fear costing you?
4. Shift from Fear to Intuition
   - ▹ Using the principles of SAGE, which choice will bring the most long-term peace, alignment, and growth—even if it feels scary to choose?
   - ▹ Suspend judgment and give yourself permission to consider this choice an actual possibility. How would it feel to choose this option?
   - ▹ If you release your attachment to outcomes and trust you can navigate whatever happens, what is your intuition telling you to choose?
   - ▹ Write down your actualized decision.
5. Take the Smallest Possible Action
   - ▹ What's the first small step you can take that will make this choice a reality?

Chapter 9

Conclusion: A New Perspective

"Always go with the choice that scares you the most, because that's the one that is going to require the most from you. Do you really want to look back on your life and see how wonderful it could have been had you not been afraid to live it?"

—CAROLINE MYSS

The root of overthinking is fear—fear of making the "wrong" choice, of failing, of being exposed as a fraud, of judgment, of not being enough. And the more attention we give that fear, the more real it becomes.

Because reality is not fixed; it's created. Created by where we place our focus, what we believe, and what we feed with our attention.

We struggle with indecision not because of the decision itself but because of the emotional weight we attach to it—the belief that one wrong move could unravel everything.

The mind craves certainty. It craves safety.

But life offers neither guarantee nor control, only opportunity.

It offers something more sacred: *choice.*

The freedom to begin again. The power to create what's next.

So the work isn't to eliminate fear.

It's to stop letting it choose for you.

Fear is not a stop sign but an invitation. It does not warn you of danger; it signals where the most meaningful growth lies. Fear is not the enemy; it's a guide. It arises not to hold you back but to point you toward what matters most. If it didn't mean something, you wouldn't feel it.

The paradox of fear is that avoiding it perpetuates it. Confronting it dissolves it. Avoiding fear means you are also avoiding everything you want. Fear stands between you and the life you desire—not as a wall, but as a test. It is not in the way; it *is* the way. The price of your dreams is fear. Nothing else.

Happiness isn't the result of self-abandonment. And personal freedom isn't something granted through the permission of others. The moment you stop searching for the "right" choice and start trusting the one that already feels right, the weight begins to lift. Not because the decision itself becomes easier, but because you stop resisting what you already know.

Those who truly love you want your authentic happiness, not your compliance. The greatest gift you can offer them is not your sacrifice but your flourishing. Perhaps, then, the bravest decision is not self-sacrifice but self-trust.

Chapter 10

The Threshold Before You

"We are the creative force of our life, and through our own decisions rather than our conditions, if we carefully learn to do certain things, we can accomplish those goals."

—STEPHEN COVEY

You've already begun to change.

Maybe quietly. Subtly. In ways even you didn't expect.

But it's unmistakable now.

The way you view indecision, the weight you've carried, the patterns you couldn't quite name—all now brought into light.

This new perspective isn't just insight; it's a transformation in motion.

You've seen the truth: that the way you've been making decisions is no longer working—not because you're broken, but because you've outgrown it. You now hold a new lens—and a new language—for choosing.

Because once you see through the lens of truth, you can't unsee it. Once you remember that you are allowed to trust yourself, you can't go back to abandoning yourself in the same way.

You've crossed a threshold and there's no uncrossing it.

But information alone doesn't change your life. Integration does.

Which is why what comes next is about embodiment. About translating what's awakened inside you into the way you move through the world. Not perfectly, but intentionally. Not for others, but finally for yourself.

The pages ahead aren't just exercises. They're your invitation to begin again—not as the person you've had to be, but as the person you're finally ready to become.

Here's what's next:

▷ **Decision-Making Principles**
Your internal compass. A distilled map of the truths you've uncovered—so that you never lose your way when old habits try to pull you back.

▷ **Discovering Yourself as a Decision-Maker**
Powerful prompts to help you uncover how you've been making choices and what it's been costing you and transform the way you choose.

▷ **Practicing TRUST**
Step-by-step guidance to help in moments where you're struggling with indecision—so you can stop spiraling, start choosing, and begin living in alignment.

▷ **Tiny Acts of Self-Trust**
Simple, playful exercises to rewire how you relate to choice—training your nervous system to respond not with fear but with clarity and confidence.

The next sections discuss how the theory becomes lived wisdom. Through practice.

The life you've longed for is no longer a distant idea. It's here, asking for your participation.

This is where it becomes real.

Now is your chance to build a life that reflects it.

Not a life built on approval.

Not a life built on fear.

But a life that feels like *home* in your soul.

This isn't just a new chapter.

It's a rediscovery of who you truly are.

You've abandoned yourself for far too long.

Now it's time to trust yourself again.

Chapter 11

Guide to Using This Book Most Effectively

When you feel lost or disconnected from clarity, return to the *Decision-Making Principles.* It's your compass—a distilled map of the deepest truths in this book. Let it center you.

When you're struggling with indecision, walk through the *TRUST exercise.* It's designed to help you move from fear to clarity, from spiraling thoughts to grounded alignment.

When you're ready to understand the patterns behind your choices, spend time in the *Discovering Yourself as a Decision-Maker* section. It will help you uncover what's been shaping your decisions and what you want to shift moving forward.

When you want to playfully practice trusting yourself in everyday moments, choose a challenge from *Tiny Acts of Self-Trust.* These low-stakes invitations will help you embody what you've learned in ways that are fun, freeing, and surprisingly powerful.

Suggested Practice

You don't need to follow a fixed sequence, but if you want to experience the deepest shifts this book can offer, following this simple plan can help you integrate the insights into your daily life and create real, lasting change:

- **Every time you find yourself overthinking a decision:**
  Review the *Decision-Making Principles* and complete the *TRUST exercise* to move from confusion to clarity.

- **Once a day:**
  Answer a prompt from *Discovering Yourself as a Decision-Maker* to better understand how you make decisions and begin transforming the way you choose.

- **Once a week:**
  Complete a *Tiny Act of Self-Trust* to gently stretch your courage and remind yourself that you can trust your inner guidance—one small choice at a time.

Scan the QR code below to download printable versions of all the key frameworks, principles, and decision-making tools from this book.

Chapter 12

Decision-Making Principles

This is a collection of the most powerful, perspective-shifting truths in this book. These aren't just concepts to understand; they are waypoints to guide you. Lenses to see differently. Anchors to return to. Reminders of the deeper wisdom you already carry.

Read through them slowly—not just with your mind, but with your heart. Notice what resonates. What expands your perspective or gently shifts the way you think? What feels like truth?

Let each principle be more than advice. Let it be a mirror reflecting the version of you that already knows what to do when you tune into yourself. Come back to this page whenever you feel uncertain. Not to find the "right" answer but to realign with who you are becoming. The version of you who trusts yourself. Who chooses from love, not fear. Who makes decisions not to avoid life but to fully live it.

Fear & Protection

1. The root of overthinking is fear.
2. You're not stuck in indecision because you don't know what to do. You're stuck because you're afraid of what you will lose if you choose wrong.
3. Fear is an indication not that something is wrong but that you are on the verge of something right.
4. Fear is not a stop sign—it's a compass pointing toward what matters most.
5. Fear is not in the way. It is the way.
6. Fear and desire are two sides of the same coin. On the other side of fear is everything you're looking for in life.
7. Fear no longer controls you the moment you decide that your peace and growth matter more than avoiding what you're afraid of.
8. Every decision is either a step into fear or a step into freedom.

Intuition & Inner Knowing

9. The mind thinks, but intuition knows.
10. The mind will convince you that you don't know what to choose even though your intuition always does.
11. The best decisions of your life will never be found in the logic of the mind. They will be felt in the intuitive knowing of your heart.

12. The clarity you seek doesn't come before making a decision. It comes from making a decision.
13. No one else has to understand your decision for it to be right for you.
14. Give yourself the permission you keep waiting for others to give you.

Growth, Alignment & Choice

15. One of the greatest powers we possess is choice.
16. There are no inherently right, wrong, or perfect decisions—only ones that are aligned or unaligned.
17. At the heart of every decision is this question: Will this contract who you are or expand who you're becoming?
18. The best decision is the one that brings the most long-term peace, alignment, and growth.
19. The purpose of life is not to get it right but to grow. The weight of the decision lifts when you realize: No matter what you choose, you're going to grow. To create a life you love, make decisions based on what you want instead of making decisions to avoid what you fear.
20. No decision is final. You can always choose again.

Self-Trust & Emotional Freedom

21. If peace requires self-betrayal, it's not peace—it's people-pleasing.
22. The people who truly love you won't need you to abandon yourself to be loved by them.
23. Most advice is other people telling you what they would do—but they cannot tell you what's right for you.
24. Your focus determines your decisions.
25. Your focus is a mental magnet. What you place your attention on is what you attract more of in your life.
26. The emotion you make a decision from is the emotion you reinforce.
27. Attention is the architect of your reality.
28. No outcome is absolutely good or bad. Every outcome contains both positive and negative consequences.
29. We have power over *how* we make decisions but not their outcomes. Who you are is determined not by what happens but by how you respond to it.
30. Peace and confidence do not come from trying to control outcomes. They come from trusting that you will be able to navigate any outcome.
31. Ultimately, it's not the outcome that defines your path. It's your response that shapes your life.

"Every decision brings with it some good, some bad, some lessons, and some luck. The only thing that's for sure is that indecision steals many years from many people who wind up wishing they'd just had the courage to leap."

—DOE ZANTAMATA

II.

Discovering Yourself as a Decision-Maker

Guided Reflections to Understand and Transform How You Choose

"At any given moment we have two options: to step forward into growth or to step back into safety."

—ABRAHAM MASLOW

Part 1: Self-Discovery

Without awareness, nothing can change. With it, everything can. This section isn't about judging your patterns; it's about seeing them. Your decision-making has been shaped by experiences, beliefs, and fears, often without your awareness. The goal isn't to fix anything immediately but to simply notice what's been guiding you.

There are **no right or wrong answers here.** Take your time, there's no rush. Approach this with curiosity, as if discovering yourself for the first time. Awareness is the first step in change. Be kind to yourself as you go through the questions. These aren't meant to overwhelm you but to help uncover the hidden forces influencing your decisions.

What you uncover may surprise you, but that's not a problem; it's a doorway. The more honest you are, the more freeing this will be. By the end, you'll see yourself—and your decisions—in a whole new light.

Before you complete the next section, respond to the following question to help you begin reflecting on your decision-making:

What are some decisions you've made recently that you found yourself overthinking? It doesn't matter if the outcome of these decisions was good or bad, what matters is how the process felt. Write them down, and they may be helpful memories to reference when answering the following questions.

Chapter 13

Revealing the Hidden Patterns

Bringing awareness to your current decision-making process.

How would you describe yourself as a decision-maker? How does decision-making typically go for you?

How much do you overthink decisions?

NOT AT ALL — INTENSELY

1 2 3 4 5

What percentage of your decisions would you say you overthink?

NONE — ALL

1 2 3 4 5

Which kinds of decisions tend to trigger overthinking and which don't?

DO	DON'T

Why do you think that is?

What does overthinking feel like for you? (Note physical and psychological symptoms.)

PHYSICAL	PSYCHOLOGICAL

What patterns do you notice in how you tend to feel and react before, during, and after making a hard decision?	BEFORE
DURING	AFTER

If someone close to you observed your decision-making, what would they see you struggling with?

Do you feel that you make better decisions when you over-think? Why or why not?

When you're struggling to make a decision, what does it usually take for you to finally make it? What gets you past the overthinking?

What would you like to change about your decision-making?

Chapter 14

The Role of Emotions

Understanding how our emotions impact our decision-making more than we might realize.

What emotions feel most present when you're making difficult decisions? Make sure to note all emotions: positive, negative, in-between.

Do you make decisions based more on fear or growth?

FEAR GROWTH

1 2 3 4 5

Why do you think that is?

How often is fear a part of your decision-making process?

NEVER ALWAYS

1 2 3 4 5

What does this fear feel like in your mind and body?

MIND	BODY

How do you feel when you make decisions from a place of fear? During the decision? After?

What are your biggest fears when making decisions?

Where do you think these fears come from? Where else do they show up in your life?

FEAR	ORIGIN	WHERE IT APPEARS

Chapter 15

The Influence of External Pressure

Uncovering how external opinions and forces affect our decisions.

Whose approval do you seek—consciously or unconsciously—when making choices? Why do you want their validation?

What do you believe will happen if you disappoint someone with your decision?

What do you think it would mean about you if you disappointed someone you cared about?

If a choice feels deeply right but might upset someone you care about, what tends to carry more weight: their comfort or your peace?

THEIR COMFORT — YOUR PEACE

1 2 3 4 5

Why do you think that is?

If disappointing them meant peace for you, would you allow it?

Where do you think this urge to please and not disappoint others comes from? Do you remember when you first felt it?

Chapter 16

Recognizing Judgment and Narratives

Revealing the internalized stories that have been shaping your choices.

What questions tend to run through your mind when you're unsure of what to choose in a decision? Do they bring clarity or more confusion?

What do you believe you must avoid at all costs when making a decision? What emotions or outcomes feel intolerable? Why do you think that is?

How do you define a "right" and "wrong" decision?

"RIGHT"

"WRONG"

Where do you think you learned these definitions from?

Are these definitions helpful? If not, how would you redefine them?

What do you think it would mean about you if you made the "wrong" decision?

Which do you believe is more trustworthy: your intuition or your logic? Why? Has following the one you tend to default to been creating the experience of life you truly want?

How much do you trust yourself when making decisions?

NOT AT ALL — COMPLETELY

1 2 3 4 5

Why do you think that is?

How often are you actually at peace with your decisions after the fact?

NEVER — ALL OF THE TIME

1 2 3 4 5

Look at your answers to the previous two questions (how much do you trust yourself / how often are you at peace). What insights emerge from looking at these two answers together?

Do you trust that you will be okay no matter the outcome of your choices? Why or why not?

How do you typically respond when the outcome of your decisions isn't what you hoped? How would you ideally like to respond to these situations?

Chapter 17

Understanding the Cost of Overthinking

Everything in life has a cost, but not everything is worth the price we're paying.

Which of these do you tend to prioritize most when making a decision?

- ○ What will make others happy
- ○ What feels safest
- ○ What seems most logical
- ○ What aligns with who you want to become

What parts of yourself do you abandon when you try to keep everyone else comfortable?

When trying to protect yourself from making a mistake, what characteristics emerge that you wish didn't?

What parts of yourself do you suppress or ignore when making decisions?

What do you gain by staying in indecision? What does it cost you?

GAIN	COST

What's the cost of constantly listening to fear when making decisions rather than trusting yourself?

Chapter 18

Reflection

Read through your responses and reflect on them from a lens of curiosity. What did you discover about yourself from your answers? Has the current way you've been approaching making decisions been helping or hurting you? What changes would you make? How would it feel to follow through with them?

Part 2: Self-Reinvention

Now that you've become aware of the invisible forces that have been influencing your decisions, you have the power to change them. The section you just completed revealed how you've been making decisions—often from fear, pressure, or a need to get it "right." The next section is about something deeper: choosing who you want to *be* as a decision-maker. Not a reactor to your life, but the architect of it.

Most of us have never paused to imagine what it would feel like to make decisions from peace, self-trust, and alignment. But that's exactly what this section will guide you to do. Once you clarify your values, your inner compass, and what truly expands you, you'll no longer need to search for the right answer. You'll become the kind of person who creates it.

Before you complete the next section, respond to the following question to help you begin envisioning what positive decision-making could look like:

What were some decisions you've made recently where you didn't experience overthinking in the decision-making process and simply trusted yourself? It doesn't matter if the outcome of these decisions was good or bad, what matters is how the process felt. Write them down, and they may be helpful memories to reference when answering the following questions.

Chapter 19

Returning to Inner Knowing

Reconnecting with the deeper guidance that has always been within you.

When you think about some of the best decisions that you've made in your life, what was the process of making them like?

Think back on a time when you saw someone make a decision that you admired. What did you admire about how they made the decision? Was there something about their decision-making you'd like to emulate?

What did you listen to or trust to make the decisions? Did those decisions come from logic or knowing? Safety or desire for growth?

What would it feel like to make decisions without fear, judgment, or pressure guiding the process?

How do you want to *feel* during and after making decisions, and what would you need to do to feel that way?

Chapter 20

Releasing Fears and Old Beliefs

Letting go of the beliefs that may have helped us get to where we are but no longer serving us.

What beliefs are you holding on to that make you continue overthinking decisions?

How would your life be different if you let them go?

How would your life be different if your decisions prioritized your personal growth rather than outcomes, external success, or validation?

What would happen if you believed all external outcomes were a by-product of internal growth? How would that change how you live your life?

If no one ever praised or criticized your choices again, how would you make decisions differently?

If time didn't feel so scarce, what would you allow yourself to choose without hesitation? How would it feel to make time for this?

How can you tell when you are acting from a place of peace, alignment, and growth instead of fear? What does it feel like in your mind, body, and heart?

If your heart could speak to your mind right now, what would it say about the version of you that overthinks decisions?

Chapter 21

Self-Trust

Rebuilding trust in your intuition, body, and truth.

How do you know when you're no longer listening to your inner truth when making a decision? What are the earliest signs?

What helps you listen to your intuition when fear is leading you in a different direction?

If fear didn't feel like a block but like a guide, where would it be trying to lead you? What is usually on the other side of fear?

What does it look like to trust yourself—not just as a feeling, but in practice?

Imagine you've made a decision and are unhappy with the outcome. What would it look like to respond to this situation from a place of nonjudgment, compassion, and flexibility instead of fear and judgment?

How would this impact your mental health and quality of life?

Chapter 22

The Actualized Self

To create the life you desire, choose based on who you're becoming, not who you've been. Rediscover your Actualized Self: the highest potential version of yourself that chooses from self-trust, not self-protection.

When you imagine the most grounded, present, and aligned version of yourself, how do they make decisions?

What questions do they ask?

What do they *not* need anymore?

If your Actualized Self were to create a set of ideal criteria to follow when making decisions, what would those be?

- ▷
- ▷
- ▷
- ▷

What are three truths your Actualized Self would want you to remember every time you face a hard decision?

1.
2.
3.

What mantras would your Actualized Self give you to help make the most aligned and expansive decisions for you?

Chapter 23

Intention Setting

Complete the sentences:

From now on, I give myself permission to make decisions that

And I give myself permission to make decisions without *(e.g., judging or blaming myself, feeling guilty, ashamed, or unworthy)*

Chapter 24

Reflection

Read through your responses and reflect on them from a lens of curiosity. What did you discover about yourself from your answers? Has the current way you've been approaching making decisions been helping or hurting you? What changes would you make? How would it feel to give yourself permission to follow through with them?

"In any moment of decision, the best thing you can do is the right thing, the next best thing is the wrong thing, and the worst thing you can do is nothing."

—THEODORE ROOSEVELT

III.
Practicing TRUST

A Step-by-Step Exercise for When You're Overthinking Decisions

"The cave you fear to enter holds the treasure you seek."

—JOSEPH CAMPBELL

Within this section, you'll find the following:

- The essential *Decision-Making Principles* designed to ground you before you complete a TRUST Decision-Making Framework exercise
- A one-page overview of SAGE—the four dimensions of an actualized decision—to remind you to make choices that bring you the greatest peace, alignment, growth, and abundance
- Five repeated TRUST Decision-Making Framework exercise pages that walk you through the practice. You can continue the exercises in a separate notebook or journal, or download a printable copy.

Suggested Practice:

When you find yourself overthinking a decision and don't know what to choose, come back to this section. Begin by reading the *Decision-Making Principles* to ground yourself in truth. Then, revisit SAGE to reconnect with what matters most. Finally, complete one TRUST Decision-Making Framework exercise to gently move from confusion to clarity. The more you practice, the more familiar it will become, until trust is no longer something you search for but something you live from.

Decision-Making Principles

This is a collection of the most powerful, perspective-shifting truths in this book. These aren't just concepts to understand; they are waypoints to guide you. Lenses to see differently. Anchors to return to. Reminders of the deeper wisdom you already carry.

Read through them slowly—not just with your mind, but with your heart. Notice what resonates. What expands your perspective or gently shifts the way you think? What feels like truth?

Let each principle be more than advice. Let it be a mirror reflecting back the version of you that already knows what to do when you tune into yourself. Come back to this page whenever you feel uncertain. Not to find the "right" answer but to realign with who you are becoming. The version of you who trusts yourself. Who chooses from love, not fear. Who makes decisions not to avoid life but to fully live it.

Fear & Protection

1. The root of overthinking is fear.
2. You're not stuck in indecision because you don't know what to do. You're stuck because you're afraid of what you will lose if you choose wrong.

3. Fear is an indication not that something is wrong but that you are on the verge of something right.
4. Fear is not a stop sign—it's a compass pointing toward what matters most.
5. Fear is not in the way. It *is* the way.
6. Fear and desire are two sides of the same coin. On the other side of fear is everything you're looking for in life.
7. Fear no longer controls you the moment you decide that your peace and growth matter more than avoiding what you're afraid of.
8. Every decision is either a step into fear or a step into freedom.

Intuition & Inner Knowing

9. The mind thinks, but intuition knows.
10. The mind will convince you that you don't know what to choose even though your intuition always does.
11. The best decisions of your life will never be found in the logic of the mind. They will be felt in the intuitive knowing of your heart.
12. The clarity you seek doesn't come before making a decision. It comes *from* making a decision.
13. No one else has to understand your decision for it to be right for you.
14. Give yourself the permission you keep waiting for others to give you.

Growth, Alignment, & Choice

15. One of the greatest powers we possess is choice.
16. There are no inherently right, wrong, or perfect decisions—only ones that are aligned or unaligned.
17. At the heart of every decision is this question: Will this contract who you are, or expand who you're becoming?
18. The best decision is the one that brings the most long-term peace, alignment, and growth.
19. The purpose of life is not to get it right but to grow. The weight of the decision lifts when you realize: No matter what you choose, you're going to grow.
20. To create a life you love, make decisions based on what you want instead of making decisions to avoid what you fear.
21. No decision is final. You can always choose again.

Self-Trust & Emotional Freedom

22. If peace requires self-betrayal, it's not peace—it's people-pleasing.
23. The people who truly love you won't need you to abandon yourself to be loved by them.
24. Most advice is other people telling you what they would do—but they cannot tell you what's right for you.
25. Your focus determines your decisions.

26. Your focus is a mental magnet. What you place your attention on is what you attract more of in your life.
27. The emotion you make a decision from is the emotion you reinforce.
28. Attention is the architect of your reality.
29. No outcome is absolutely good or bad. Every outcome contains both positive and negative consequences.
30. We have power over *how* we make decisions, but not their outcomes. Who you are is determined not by what happens but by how you respond to it. Peace and confidence do not come from trying to control outcomes. They come from trusting that you will be able to navigate any outcome.
31. Ultimately, it's not the outcome that defines your path. It's your response that shapes your life.

The Dimensions of an Actualized Decision

SAGE

An actualized decision is a choice made not from fear, pressure, or the need for approval but from self-trust, presence, alignment, and love. It is the decision that brings the greatest peace and growth, not because the outcome is guaranteed, but because of who you become by choosing it.

Serenity—Which choice will give me the deepest long-term peace?
Alignment—Which choice aligns with who I want to become?
Growth—Which choice expands me the most?
Emotion—Which choice is driven by love and abundance rather than fear?

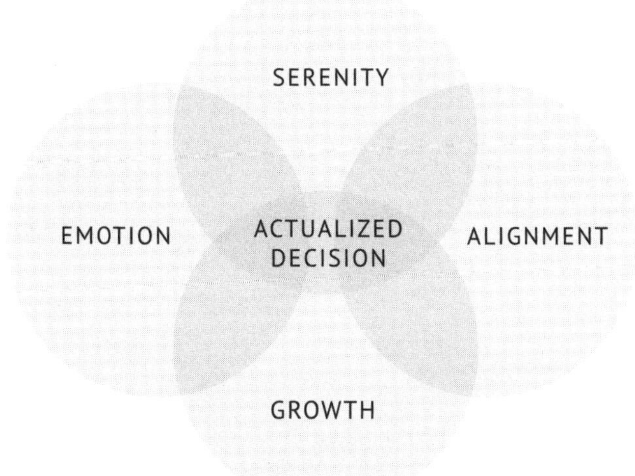

"You cannot swim for new horizons until you have courage to lose sight of the shore."

—WILLIAM FAULKNER

TRUST Decision-Making Framework

The TRUST Framework is a tool to help you make the most actualized decision—the one that brings the greatest peace, growth, and alignment. Instead of falling into the trap of chasing the "right" choice, it guides you out of overthinking and into deeper self-trust, helping you choose from intuition so that your life is shaped by your truth, not fears. Because this is an exercise you'll want to come back to on a regular basis, I recommend you write your responses in a separate notebook or journal. If you'd like a printable copy of the TRUST Decision-Making Framework, you can download one from my website at josephnguyen.org/resources

Take five deep breaths.

Regulate the nervous system by taking five slow, deep breaths. Try the two-to-one breathing technique: inhale for four seconds, and exhale for eight.

Reveal the root decision.

State the decision you are facing in one clear sentence. Don't include the possible outcomes or emotions, just the decision at hand. What event prompted this decision?

Uncover the fear and its cost.

What are you afraid might happen if you choose wrong? What do you worry that choosing wrong would mean about you?

What is this fear costing you?

Shift from fear to intuition.

Using the principles of SAGE, which choice will bring the most long-term peace, alignment, and growth—even if it feels scary to choose?

Suspend judgment and give yourself permission to consider this choice an actual possibility. How would it feel to choose this option?

If you release your attachment to outcomes and trust you can navigate whatever happens, what is your intuition telling you to choose?

Write down your actualized decision:

Take the smallest possible action.

What's the first small step you can take that will make this choice a reality?

Reflection

How did this decision feel? What did you learn about your thoughts, patterns, and fears? What did you learn about what helps you break through overthinking?

TRUST Decision-Making Framework

Take five deep breaths.

Regulate the nervous system by taking five slow, deep breaths. Try the two-to-one breathing technique: inhale for four seconds, and exhale for eight.

Reveal the root decision.

State the decision you are facing in one clear sentence. Don't include the possible outcomes or emotions, just the decision at hand. What event prompted this decision?

Uncover the fear and its cost.

What are you afraid might happen if you choose wrong? What do you worry that choosing wrong would mean about you?

What is this fear costing you?

Shift from fear to intuition.

Using the principles of SAGE, which choice will bring the most long-term peace, alignment, and growth—even if it feels scary to choose?

Suspend judgment and give yourself permission to consider this choice an actual possibility. How would it feel to choose this option?

If you release your attachment to outcomes and trust you can navigate whatever happens, what is your intuition telling you to choose?

Write down your actualized decision:

Take the smallest possible action.

What's the first small step you can take that will make this choice a reality?

Reflection

How did this decision feel? What did you learn about your thoughts, patterns, and fears? What did you learn about what helps you break through overthinking?

TRUST Decision-Making Framework

Take five deep breaths.

Regulate the nervous system by taking five slow, deep breaths. Try the two-to-one breathing technique: inhale for four seconds, and exhale for eight.

Reveal the root decision.

State the decision you are facing in one clear sentence. Don't include the possible outcomes or emotions, just the decision at hand. What event prompted this decision?

Uncover the fear and its cost.

What are you afraid might happen if you choose wrong? What do you worry that choosing wrong would mean about you?

What is this fear costing you?

Shift from fear to intuition.

Using the principles of SAGE, which choice will bring the most long-term peace, alignment, and growth—even if it feels scary to choose?

Suspend judgment and give yourself permission to consider this choice an actual possibility. How would it feel to choose this option?

If you release your attachment to outcomes and trust you can navigate whatever happens, what is your intuition telling you to choose?

Write down your actualized decision:

Take the smallest possible action.

What's the first small step you can take that will make this choice a reality?

Reflection

How did this decision feel? What did you learn about your thoughts, patterns, and fears? What did you learn about what helps you break through overthinking?

TRUST Decision-Making Framework

Take five deep breaths.

Regulate the nervous system by taking five slow, deep breaths. Try the two-to-one breathing technique: inhale for four seconds, and exhale for eight.

Reveal the root decision.

State the decision you are facing in one clear sentence. Don't include the possible outcomes or emotions, just the decision at hand. What event prompted this decision?

Uncover the fear and its cost.

What are you afraid might happen if you choose wrong? What do you worry that choosing wrong would mean about you?

What is this fear costing you?

Shift from fear to intuition.

Using the principles of SAGE, which choice will bring the most long-term peace, alignment, and growth—even if it feels scary to choose?

Suspend judgment and give yourself permission to consider this choice an actual possibility. How would it feel to choose this option?

If you release your attachment to outcomes and trust you can navigate whatever happens, what is your intuition telling you to choose?

Write down your actualized decision:

Take the smallest possible action.

What's the first small step you can take that will make this choice a reality?

Reflection

How did this decision feel? What did you learn about your thoughts, patterns, and fears? What did you learn about what helps you break through overthinking?

TRUST Decision-Making Framework

Take five deep breaths.

Regulate the nervous system by taking five slow, deep breaths. Try the two-to-one breathing technique: inhale for four seconds, and exhale for eight.

Reveal the root decision.

State the decision you are facing in one clear sentence. Don't include the possible outcomes or emotions, just the decision at hand. What event prompted this decision?

Uncover the fear and its cost.

What are you afraid might happen if you choose wrong? What do you worry that choosing wrong would mean about you?

What is this fear costing you?

Shift from fear to intuition.

Using the principles of SAGE, which choice will bring the most long-term peace, alignment, and growth—even if it feels scary to choose?

Suspend judgment and give yourself permission to consider this choice an actual possibility. How would it feel to choose this option?

If you release your attachment to outcomes and trust you can navigate whatever happens, what is your intuition telling you to choose?

Write down your actualized decision:

Take the smallest possible action.

What's the first small step you can take that will make this choice a reality?

Reflection

How did this decision feel? What did you learn about your thoughts, patterns, and fears? What did you learn about what helps you break through overthinking?

Reflection

Take a moment and go through the last five exercises you filled out and notice the patterns, shifts, and insights that have emerged. This is your chance to pause and witness what's changing and growing—not just in your decisions, but in you. Let this be a space to become mindful of what's working, what's ready to be released, and what's asking for more of your trust.

Progress Check-In

How much was overthinking present in these decisions?

CONSTANTLY NOT AT ALL

1 2 3 4 5

How much did you trust yourself in these decisions compared to before this process?

MUCH LESS MUCH MORE

1 2 3 4 5

How much were you able to trust that you'd be able to handle the outcomes of the decisions, even if they weren't the ones you desired?

MUCH LESS COMPLETELY

1 2 3 4 5

How different does your decision-making feel now compared to before this process?

NO CHANGE COMPLETELY TRANSFORMED

1 2 3 4 5

Self-Reflection

Which decision felt the hardest? Did you recognize any patterns in your thoughts or fears in those moments? What insights can you draw from these experiences?

What makes overthinking worse when making decisions? What helps you let go of overthinking decisions and trust yourself? How can you bring more of that into future decisions?

What did it feel like in the moments when you followed your intuition rather than fear? What did you learn from those experiences?

If this page marked the end of one old belief, story, or way of being, what would it be? What are you ready to leave behind?

How have you felt your decision-making change over the course of working through these exercises?

What do you want to remember the next time you're facing a challenging decision that would help you most?

"You may not control all the events that happen to you, but you can decide not to be reduced by them."

—MAYA ANGELOU

IV.
Tiny Acts of Self-Trust

Mini-Decision-Making Experiments to Help You Stop Overthinking and Start Trusting Yourself Again

"The greatest mistake you can make in life is to be continually fearing that you will make one."

—ELBERT HUBBARD

This section contains a series of insightful miniexperiments designed to be both playful and profound—inviting you into everyday scenarios where you can safely practice trusting yourself and your intuition.

While knowledge comes through understanding, wisdom is born through experience. These challenges help translate what you've learned in the book into embodied insight, turning ideas into inner shifts and reflections into new ways of being. What may seem like a small act on the surface often becomes a powerful catalyst beneath it. You might be surprised by how these subtle choices begin to reshape how you see yourself, how you make decisions, and how deeply you're capable of living in alignment with who you truly are.

“The privilege of a lifetime is to become who you truly are.”

—CARL JUNG

Flip a Coin and Follow the Feeling

Think of a decision you're currently facing. Assign heads and tails to the two options, then flip the coin. But before you look at the result, pause. Ask yourself: *What do I hope it lands on?* Just noticing your answer can be revealing.

Now look at the coin and see the result. How do you feel about the option that was chosen for you? Are you relieved? Disappointed? Surprised? Your reaction reveals the answer you subconsciously wanted before your mind had a chance to overanalyze or second-guess.

This experiment isn't about leaving your choice to chance. It's about learning to trust the truth already within you.

Planning

Use this space to plan out how you will complete this exercise. What decision will you use it for? If your mind tries to talk you out of it, what truth can you remind yourself of in that moment to stay committed to this experiment?

Reflection

Use this space to reflect on how the experiment went. How did it go? What surprised you? How did it feel to complete it? What did you learn about yourself through the experience? What insights do you want to take from this that would be most helpful for future decisions?

Go with Your Gut for Food

The next time you're at a restaurant (or deciding what to eat), choose the first thing that genuinely speaks to you before scanning every option, comparing, or calculating what's "best." Let yourself order without overthinking, without needing it to be perfect.

This exercise is a practice of trusting your gut—literally. Notice how it feels to honor your first instinct instead of trying to overanalyze the choice. Even something as simple as choosing a meal can be a doorway to more ease, more self-trust, and more presence with what's in front of you.

Planning

Use this space to plan out how you will complete this exercise. When will you do it? If your mind tries to talk you out of it, what truth can you remind yourself of in that moment to stay committed to this experiment?

Reflection

Use this space to reflect on how the experiment went. How did it go? What surprised you? How did it feel to complete it? What did you learn about yourself through the experience? What insights do you want to take from this that would be most helpful for future decisions?

Follow a Tiny Spark

Say yes to something small that sparks your curiosity or excitement—something that feels oddly compelling, even if it doesn't make logical sense. Maybe it's a book you feel pulled toward, a side street you've never explored, or an idea that lights you up for no obvious reason.

This experiment isn't about being practical, it's about honoring energy over logic and learning to listen to what you *want* to do instead of what you think you *should* do. When you follow those quiet, expansive sparks, you create space for joy, surprise, and growth. Over time, this practice teaches you that what feels alive is often far more worthwhile than what merely makes sense.

Planning

Use this space to plan out how you will complete this exercise. When will you do it? If your mind tries to talk you out of it, what truth can you remind yourself of in that moment to stay committed to this experiment?

Reflection

Use this space to reflect on how the experiment went. How did it go? What surprised you? How did it feel to complete it? What did you learn about yourself through the experience? What insights do you want to take from this that would be most helpful for future decisions?

"The risk of a wrong decision is preferable to the terror of indecision."

—MAIMONIDES

Choose Without Research

For one small decision today—what to buy, where to eat, which option to pick—resist the urge to read reviews, check ratings, or ask for anyone else's opinion. Just pause, tune in, and choose what feels right in the moment without gathering more data. Then observe *how* you feel, both before and after the choice. Notice whether peace, tension, or clarity arises, not from what you chose, but from how you chose it. This is a gentle way to practice trusting your internal compass before outsourcing your knowing to the outside world.

Planning

Use this space to plan out how you will complete this exercise. When will you do it? If your mind tries to talk you out of it, what truth can you remind yourself of in that moment to stay committed to this experiment?

Reflection

Use this space to reflect on how the experiment went. How did it go? What surprised you? How did it feel to complete it? What did you learn about yourself through the experience? What insights do you want to take from this that would be most helpful for future decisions?

Walk Without a Destination

Set aside 15 minutes to take a walk with no phone, no plan, and no destination. Don't map the route or decide in advance where you'll go. Just step outside and see where your feet take you. Follow whatever path calls to you, even if it doesn't "make sense." Let the walk be aimless, curious, and unhurried. Look at things as if you are seeing them through the eyes of a child for the first time.

During the walk, practice presence. Gently release any thoughts about what you need to do next. You don't have to solve anything or be productive right now. This is a practice of letting life unfold without needing to control it. Often, the moments that we remember most aren't the ones we planned but the ones where we were the most present. When life stops being a means to an end and becomes a joy in itself, peace finds its way back in. Notice how you feel during and after. What shifts when you no longer have anywhere to be but here?

Planning

Use this space to plan out how you will complete this exercise. When will you do it? If your mind tries to talk you out of it, what truth can you remind yourself of in that moment to stay committed to this experiment?

Reflection

Use this space to reflect on how the experiment went. How did it go? What surprised you? How did it feel to complete it? What did you learn about yourself through the experience? What insights do you want to take from this that would be most helpful for future decisions?

Ask for What You Need

Choose one small need you usually ignore or suppress and express it to someone else. It could be as simple as, "Can we pause for a minute?" "I need a little space," "Can we reschedule?" or "I'd actually prefer this instead."

It doesn't have to be dramatic. It just has to be honest. Each time you voice a need—especially in the small moments—you affirm to yourself that your well-being matters and that you can make choices that honor it. Self-trust deepens when you stop abandoning yourself in the name of staying connected and start building connections that include you, too.

Planning

Use this space to plan out how you will complete this exercise. When will you do it? If your mind tries to talk you out of it, what truth can you remind yourself of in that moment to stay committed to this experiment?

Reflection

Use this space to reflect on how the experiment went. How did it go? What surprised you? How did it feel to complete it? What did you learn about yourself through the experience? What insights do you want to take from this that would be most helpful for future decisions?

Write Without Editing

Set a timer for five minutes and free-write on a piece of paper about a decision or feeling you've been struggling with. As you write, don't erase, don't censor. Let the words come exactly as they are: messy, tangled, unsure. Often, the truth spills out when we stop trying to say it perfectly.

Once it's all on the page, take a breath and read what you wrote. There's often a surprising sense of relief that comes when the noise in your head becomes something you can see with your eyes. What stands out to you? What patterns or insights emerge? And most importantly, what is your intuition whispering beneath the overthinking?

Planning

Use this space to plan out how you will complete this exercise. When will you do it? If your mind tries to talk you out of it, what truth can you remind yourself of in that moment to stay committed to this experiment?

Reflection

Use this space to reflect on how the experiment went. How did it go? What surprised you? How did it feel to complete it? What did you learn about yourself through the experience? What insights do you want to take from this that would be most helpful for future decisions?

"There is freedom waiting for you, on the breezes of the sky. And you ask 'What if I fall?' Oh but my darling, what if you fly?"

—ERIN HANSON

Follow Your Inner Child

When we were young, we followed what felt fun, exciting, or curious without needing a reason why. We played, explored, created, and changed our minds freely. But somewhere along the way, many of us traded that joy for practicality and logic. We began suppressing the parts of ourselves that once made us feel alive. And then we wondered why everything started to feel so serious and heavy.

This experiment is simple: give yourself permission to do one thing today that your inner child would love. Something that may not be "productive" or make sense to anyone else. Maybe it's returning to a hobby you once loved, rewatching a movie you remember fondly, dancing around your living room to a favorite song from when you were growing up, or pulling out old photos, drawings, or letters and letting yourself remember who you were before the world told you who to be.

It doesn't need to take your whole day. But offering even a moment to this part of you—without judgment or justification—can nourish your spirit in ways logic never will. What would make your inner child smile today? Let yourself have that. Then notice how it feels to come alive again.

Planning

Use this space to plan out how you will complete this exercise. When will you do it? If your mind tries to talk you out of it, what truth can you remind yourself of in that moment to stay committed to this experiment?

Reflection

Use this space to reflect on how the experiment went. How did it go? What surprised you? How did it feel to complete it? What did you learn about yourself through the experience? What insights do you want to take from this that would be most helpful for future decisions?

Ask Yourself Instead of Someone Else

The next time you feel the urge to ask for someone else's opinion, pause. Before reaching out, turn inward and ask: Do I really need an outside perspective? What do I already know? What would I choose if I fully trusted myself?

This isn't about always having the right answer, it's about practicing the art of being your own source. Every time you check in with yourself first, you strengthen the quiet muscle of self-trust. Over time, it becomes easier to hear your voice—even when the world is loud.

Planning

Use this space to plan out how you will complete this exercise. When will you do it? If your mind tries to talk you out of it, what truth can you remind yourself of in that moment to stay committed to this experiment?

Reflection

Use this space to reflect on how the experiment went. How did it go? What surprised you? How did it feel to complete it? What did you learn about yourself through the experience? What insights do you want to take from this that would be most helpful for future decisions?

The Courage to Say No

Say a gentle no to something small today—something you'd normally say yes to out of guilt or habit. Maybe it's continuing a text conversation you don't have energy for or agreeing to a minor favor you don't want to do. This time, don't overexplain or justify. Simply say, *"I'm not able to right now,"* and let that be enough. Then, give yourself full permission to not feel guilty—for protecting your energy, for honoring your peace, for listening to yourself.

Afterward, pause and reflect. How did you feel right before saying no? And how did you feel after? What shifted when you allowed yourself to release the guilt?

Planning

Use this space to plan out how you will complete this exercise. When will you do it? If your mind tries to talk you out of it, what truth can you remind yourself of in that moment to stay committed to this experiment?

Reflection

Use this space to reflect on how the experiment went. How did it go? What surprised you? How did it feel to complete it? What did you learn about yourself through the experience? What insights do you want to take from this that would be most helpful for future decisions?

Choose Presence over Productivity

Set aside one hour today to be completely unproductive—on purpose. No multitasking, no crossing things off a list, no optimizing. Just sit, breathe, sip tea, lie on the floor, stare out the window, go for a walk, visit a park, and. Let yourself be.

This isn't about abandoning your responsibilities. It's about remembering that your worth isn't tied to how much you accomplish. Giving yourself even one hour of true rest can restore the energy, clarity, and presence you bring to everything else. Let this be your quiet reminder that everything will still get done, but from a place that feels less stressful and more grounded.

Planning

Use this space to plan out how you will complete this exercise. When will you do it? If your mind tries to talk you out of it, what truth can you remind yourself of in that moment to stay committed to this experiment?

Reflection

Use this space to reflect on how the experiment went. How did it go? What surprised you? How did it feel to complete it? What did you learn about yourself through the experience? What insights do you want to take from this that would be most helpful for future decisions?

Voice a Preference Out Loud

The next time someone asks what you'd like—where to sit, what to eat, what to do—voice your preference instead of defaulting to what others want. Don't overthink it. Don't minimize it. Just say what you'd genuinely prefer, even if it's as simple as, "*I'd rather sit over here,*" or "*I'd love to do this instead.*"

Most of the time, it's not an inconvenience, it's just a choice. And giving yourself permission to choose without guilt is a powerful act of self-trust. Every time you allow yourself to take up space, you reinforce this truth: your needs matter just as much as anyone else's.

Planning

Use this space to plan out how you will complete this exercise. When will you do it? If your mind tries to talk you out of it, what truth can you remind yourself of in that moment to stay committed to this experiment?

Reflection

Use this space to reflect on how the experiment went. How did it go? What surprised you? How did it feel to complete it? What did you learn about yourself through the experience? What insights do you want to take from this that would be most helpful for future decisions?

Follow Through on a Promise to Yourself

Choose one small but meaningful thing you've been wanting to do—move your body, rest without guilt, make time for a creative hobby—and write it down as a promise to yourself: "Today, I will…"

Then do it. Not because you have to, but because you said you would. It doesn't matter how big or small the action is. What matters is that you honored your word to yourself.

Self-trust isn't built through achievement; it's built through showing up for yourself again and again in quiet, consistent ways. This is how you become someone you can count on.

Planning

Use this space to plan out how you will complete this exercise. When will you do it? If your mind tries to talk you out of it, what truth can you remind yourself of in that moment to stay committed to this experiment?

Reflection

Use this space to reflect on how the experiment went. How did it go? What surprised you? How did it feel to complete it? What did you learn about yourself through the experience? What insights do you want to take from this that would be most helpful for future decisions?

"You don't have to see the whole staircase,
just take the first step."

—MARTIN LUTHER KING JR.

Break One Tiny Habit (on Purpose)

What's one small habit you've been repeating that no longer feels aligned with who you want to be? Something that drains you, distracts you, or keeps you stuck on autopilot? Today, interrupt that pattern just once. Step outside instead of reaching for your phone. Pause before responding how you usually would. Allow yourself to simply be bored and rest for a bit without needing to distract yourself. Do the opposite of what the old pattern expects.

You don't have to overhaul your life, just create a single microdisruption. Notice how it feels to *choose* rather than operate by default. Even the smallest break in routine can remind you: you are the one steering this life. You can shift, even slightly, toward more peace, more presence, more intention.

Planning

Use this space to plan out how you will complete this exercise. When will you do it? If your mind tries to talk you out of it, what truth can you remind yourself of in that moment to stay committed to this experiment?

Reflection

Use this space to reflect on how the experiment went. How did it go? What surprised you? How did it feel to complete it? What did you learn about yourself through the experience? What insights do you want to take from this that would be most helpful for future decisions?

Set an 80% Rule

Today, choose one decision to make when you feel only 80% sure of your choice and let that be enough. Don't chase the final 20% of certainty. You don't need all the information to move forward. You only need enough.

Waiting for absolute clarity often leads to inaction, not better choices. This experiment invites you to act with what you know now and trust yourself to adjust as you go. Progress comes not from perfection, but from choosing and learning in motion.

Planning

Use this space to plan out how you will complete this exercise. When will you do it? If your mind tries to talk you out of it, what truth can you remind yourself of in that moment to stay committed to this experiment?

Reflection

Use this space to reflect on how the experiment went. How did it go? What surprised you? How did it feel to complete it? What did you learn about yourself through the experience? What insights do you want to take from this that would be most helpful for future decisions?

Delay the Decision on Purpose

Choose a decision you feel pressure to make and deliberately delay it for 24 hours. Not to procrastinate or ruminate, but to pause, on purpose. Give yourself full permission not to think about it until tomorrow. No spiraling, no problem-solving. Just space.

When the next day arrives, return to the decision with fresh eyes. What's different now? Has anything shifted? Your clarity, your emotional state, the decision itself? Notice what changes when you trust time to clarify instead of scrambling to fix. Sometimes the pressure lifts simply because you allowed it to.

Planning

Use this space to plan out how you will complete this exercise. When will you do it? If your mind tries to talk you out of it, what truth can you remind yourself of in that moment to stay committed to this experiment?

Reflection

Use this space to reflect on how the experiment went. How did it go? What surprised you? How did it feel to complete it? What did you learn about yourself through the experience? What insights do you want to take from this that would be most helpful for future decisions?

"Once you make a decision, the universe conspires to make it happen."

—RALPH WALDO EMERSON

Take Aligned Action Before You Feel "Ready"

Choose one small action that moves you closer to something you care about. Send the message. Open the document. Make the call. Whatever it is, do it before you feel fully certain or ready.

Most of us wait for clarity like it's a permission slip. But clarity is often what follows the choice, not what precedes it. The more you try to think your way into certainty, the further away it drifts. Action reveals what overthinking hides. You learn faster by doing. You adjust more easily in motion. And some doors only appear once you're already walking.

Planning

Use this space to plan out how you will complete this exercise. When will you do it? If your mind tries to talk you out of it, what truth can you remind yourself of in that moment to stay committed to this experiment?

Reflection

Use this space to reflect on how the experiment went. How did it go? What surprised you? How did it feel to complete it? What did you learn about yourself through the experience? What insights do you want to take from this that would be most helpful for future decisions?

Do One Thing for Yourself

Do one thing for yourself just because you want to. Not because it's productive. Not because it makes sense. Not because someone else asked or approved. But simply because you want to.

Today, give yourself permission to do something you've been longing to do—something small or big that you've talked yourself out of, convinced yourself was silly, indulgent, or unnecessary. Maybe it felt like a waste of time or money. But if it brings even a flicker of joy, that's more than enough of a reason.

When you stop suppressing the part of you that craves play, adventure, beauty, or rest, you learn to listen to your desires again. You begin making space for aliveness—for joy, for wonder, for the kind of moments that don't need to be useful to be meaningful.

Let today be a gift to yourself, for no other reason than because your desire matters.

Planning

Use this space to plan out how you will complete this exercise. When will you do it? If your mind tries to talk you out of it, what truth can you remind yourself of in that moment to stay committed to this experiment?

Reflection

Use this space to reflect on how the experiment went. How did it go? What surprised you? How did it feel to complete it? What did you learn about yourself through the experience? What insights do you want to take from this that would be most helpful for future decisions?

Ask a Question You're Scared to Know the Answer To

Bring to mind a question you've been avoiding—something you've been too afraid to ask out loud, whether in conversation, in your journal, or quietly within your own heart. Let this moment be your permission to finally ask it.

We often avoid these questions because we fear the answer might hurt, catalyze change, or reveal a truth we're not ready to face. But most of the time, the fear of the answer is louder than the answer itself. And when we finally face it, we realize that we can handle more than we thought.

You don't need to force clarity or action right away. Just begin by asking and holding space for whatever comes up. This is how we build self-trust—not by controlling the answers, but by being willing to hear them and knowing we can handle whatever they may be.

Planning

Use this space to plan out how you will complete this exercise. When will you do it? If your mind tries to talk you out of it, what truth can you remind yourself of in that moment to stay committed to this experiment?

Reflection

Use this space to reflect on how the experiment went. How did it go? What surprised you? How did it feel to complete it? What did you learn about yourself through the experience? What insights do you want to take from this that would be most helpful for future decisions?

A Day of Trusting Your Intuition

For one full day, make a conscious commitment: whenever a decision comes up—big or small—choose to follow your intuition rather than overanalyzing. Don't spiral into pros and cons. Don't wait for certainty. Just feel for what resonates, and go with it. Of course, stay safe and grounded; this isn't about being reckless. But most choices we face aren't life-threatening; they're invitations to build trust with ourselves. As the day unfolds, pay close attention to how you feel both during and after each decision. Does acting on intuition bring a sense of freedom or unease? Does it spark relief, joy, or clarity? How does it feel to go a day living your life intuitively rather than analytically?

Planning

Use this space to plan out how you will complete this exercise. When will you do it? If your mind tries to talk you out of it, what truth can you remind yourself of in that moment to stay committed to this experiment?

Reflection

Use this space to reflect on how the experiment went. How did it go? What surprised you? How did it feel to complete it? What did you learn about yourself through the experience? What insights do you want to take from this that would be most helpful for future decisions?

Create Your Own Mini-Experiment

Design a small experiment that might help you overthink your decisions a little less. It could be something out of your usual routine—a tiny stretch beyond your comfort zone—or a bigger leap you've quietly wanted to take but haven't given yourself permission to try.

Let it be something that doesn't need to make sense to anyone else. Maybe it has no obvious purpose. Maybe it doesn't feel "productive." But if it brings even a little peace, play, or freedom to your day, that's more than enough.

This is your space to choose. What's one thing you'd love to try, just for you?

Planning

Use this space to plan out how you will complete this exercise. When will you do it? If your mind tries to talk you out of it, what truth can you remind yourself of in that moment to stay committed to this experiment?

Reflection

Use this space to reflect on how the experiment went. How did it go? What surprised you? How did it feel to complete it? What did you learn about yourself through the experience? What insights do you want to take from this that would be most helpful for future decisions?

Create Your Own Mini-Experiment

Design a small experiment that might help you overthink your decisions a little less. It could be something out of your usual routine—a tiny stretch beyond your comfort zone—or a bigger leap you've quietly wanted to take but haven't given yourself permission to try.

Let it be something that doesn't need to make sense to anyone else. Maybe it has no obvious purpose. Maybe it doesn't feel "productive." But if it brings even a little peace, play, or freedom to your day, that's more than enough.

This is your space to choose. What's one thing you'd love to try, just for you?

Planning

Use this space to plan out how you will complete this exercise. When will you do it? If your mind tries to talk you out of it, what truth can you remind yourself of in that moment to stay committed to this experiment?

Reflection

Use this space to reflect on how the experiment went. How did it go? What surprised you? How did it feel to complete it? What did you learn about yourself through the experience? What insights do you want to take from this that would be most helpful for future decisions?

Create Your Own Mini-Experiment

Design a small experiment that might help you overthink your decisions a little less. It could be something out of your usual routine—a tiny stretch beyond your comfort zone—or a bigger leap you've quietly wanted to take but haven't given yourself permission to try.

Let it be something that doesn't need to make sense to anyone else. Maybe it has no obvious purpose. Maybe it doesn't feel "productive." But if it brings even a little peace, play, or freedom to your day, that's more than enough.

This is your space to choose. What's one thing you'd love to try, just for you?

Planning

Use this space to plan out how you will complete this exercise. When will you do it? If your mind tries to talk you out of it, what truth can you remind yourself of in that moment to stay committed to this experiment?

Reflection

Use this space to reflect on how the experiment went. How did it go? What surprised you? How did it feel to complete it? What did you learn about yourself through the experience? What insights do you want to take from this that would be most helpful for future decisions?

What Should You Read Next?

Thank you from the bottom of my heart for taking the time to read this book. If you enjoyed it, I highly recommend checking out my first book, *Don't Believe Everything You Think (Expanded Edition)*, which explores how to break free from anxiety and self-doubt.

Every week, I share a new piece of writing through my "Nuggets of Wisdom" newsletter, which contains one simple, perspective-shifting idea to expand your mind and help you find more peace, joy, and abundance.

Subscribers are also the first to hear about my newest books and projects.

Join our community of seekers and sign up for my newsletter at josephnguyen.org/newsletter.

Or you may sign up by scanning the QR code below: